IMAGES OF ENGLAND

GUILDFORD

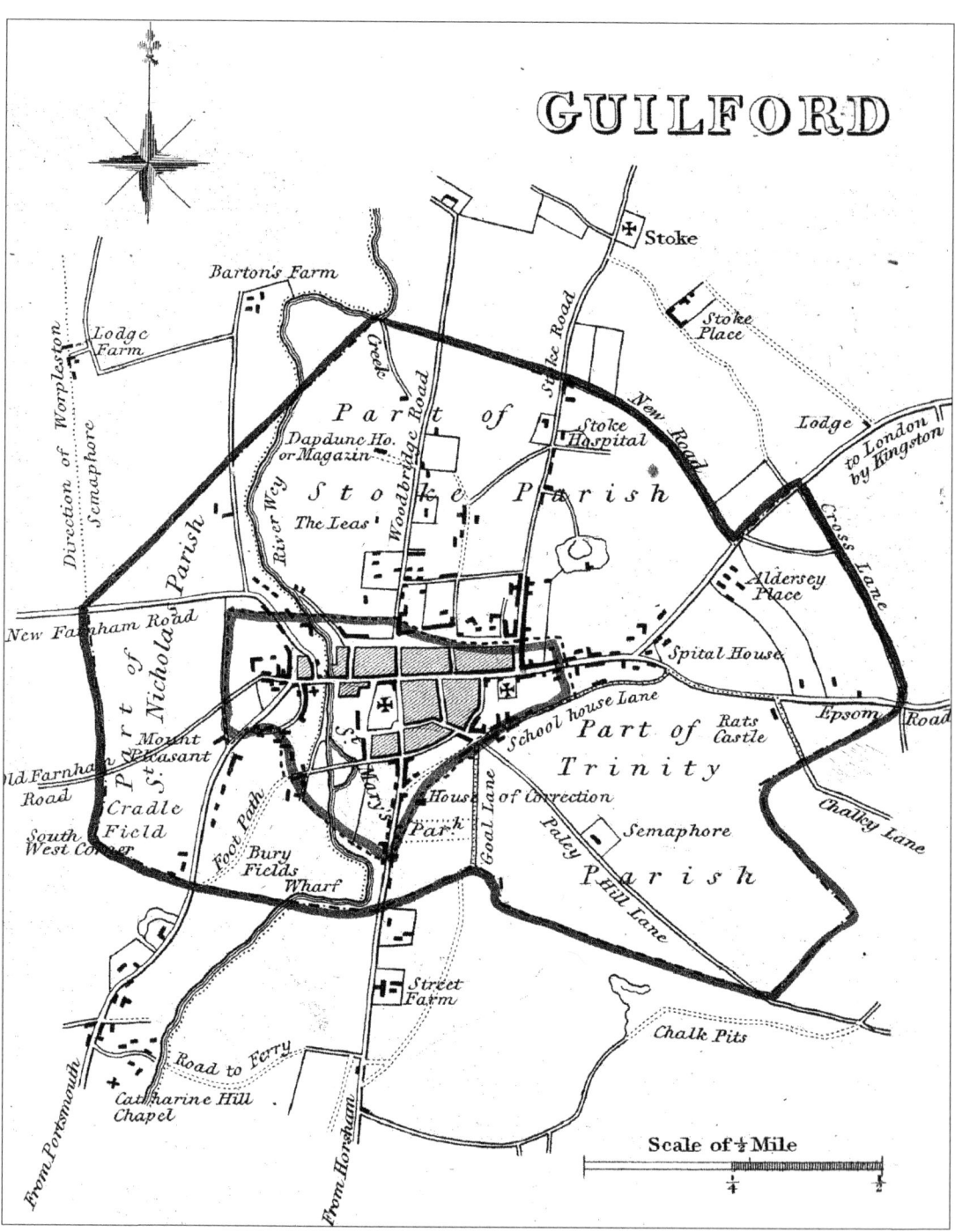

GUILFORD

Stoke

Stoke Place

Barton's Farm

Lodge Farm

Direction of Worpleston Semaphore

Creek

Part of Stoke Parish

Dapdunc Ho. or Magazin

Stoke Road

New Road

Lodge

to London by Kingston

Cross Lane

Stoke Hospital

Woodbridge Road

River Wey

The Leas

Part of St. Nicholas Parish

Aldersey Place

New Farnham Road

Spital House

Epsom Road

St. Mary's

School house Lane

Rats Castle

Part of Trinity

Chalky Lane

Old Farnham Road

Mount Pleasant

Park

Goal Lane

House of Correction

Semaphore

Cradle Field

Parish

South West Corner

Foot Path

Bury Fields

Wharf

Paley Hill Lane

Chalk Pits

Street Farm

Road to Ferry

From Portsmouth

Catharine Hill Chapel

From Horsham

Scale of ½ Mile

IMAGES OF ENGLAND

GUILDFORD

PHILIP HUTCHINSON

TEMPUS

Frontispiece: Guildford (commonly misspelt as 'Guilford') in 1835 shortly after construction of The Hog's Back and showing the 'old' and 'new' Farnham roads.

First published 2006

Tempus Publishing Limited
The Mill, Brimscombe Port,
Stroud, Gloucestershire, GL5 2QG
www.tempus-publishing.com

British Library Cataloguing in Publication Data.
A catalogue record for this book is available from the British Library.

ISBN 0 7524 4203 1

Typesetting and origination by Tempus Publishing Limited.
Printed in Great Britain.

Contents

Acknowledgements

The amount of people I have to thank for their help in putting this book together is vast. I would like to dedicate my efforts to all of them, and to the spirit of sharing they have demonstrated.

Firstly, I would like to thank those collectors and historians who have helped me above all others. Here's to David Rose, Stan Newman, Jo Harle (who loaned several of the images of the Royal Grammar School and Stoke Park), Julian Morgan (again, who gave kind permission to use several old photographs in his collection), Chris Quinn (likewise) and Lucy McCorkindale, who sorted out some snapshots from her family archives which she wrongly assumed might not interest anyone else!

Thanks are also due to David Pyle for his kind donation of a collection of images of Guildford in 1963 he had inherited and to Martin Loader, Maureen Powles, Bev Williams, Judy Oliver, Amanda Bawden and Andrew McGarrigle, Carol Ovens, Mark Wingham and Richard Winslade – all of them eBayers of merit – for their donations of single images I couldn't acquire.

Finally, there were glaring gaps in my knowledge to put some accurate captions with a few of the shots in the book. To this end I wish to thank David Peters, Bob Ellison, Brendan Cumberbirch, Angie Wallberg, John Janaway, Carol Brown, Pete Phillips, Jackie and David Marjoram and Geraldine Middleton-Stewart for their advice.

My apologies if I have missed anyone out who helped me with my research. Likewise, my apologies if I have used any images in the book which you may recognise as being under your copyright. None of the photos here, except those I have had clearance for, have a provenance I could trace to a previous owner.

Introduction

It is a sunny afternoon in June. I sit near the banks of the River Wey in The White House pub, in the company of several local experts and collectors, all of whom have kindly agreed to my request to meet up and look through my Guildford collection to help me choose images for this book. I think how good it is of them to give up their time to assist me. It becomes apparent that true collectors and historians are not those that take rare images and documents from the marketplace and hoard them away, only to be seen again on payment of a fee or – worse still – kept under lock and key for good. The true enthusiast is only too happy to share what they have with others. They like to bring back memories, to attract a new audience and – yes – to show off their collections.

I have lived in Guildford for some years now but am not a Guildfordian by birth. However, I like to think I have been adopted as an 'honorary' Guildfordian and have been welcomed into the ranks of the Guildford Anoraks – that group of people with an obsession with the history of the town.

My collection began when I started working at Guildford Castle Keep in 1994. I started to accrue postcards of the keep and grounds as they looked in years gone by, encouraged by John Black, my boss at the time. When I moved to Guildford I branched out that collection. In January 2004 I finally got a computer and discovered eBay within days. This on-line auction house has occupied a great deal of my time (and money!) ever since and it is through this and postcard fairs that I have obtained most of my Guildford images.

I found most people to be remarkably helpful when I began to put this book together. Yes, there are eBay sellers and buyers who would ignore requests for help but for every one of them there would be two who would be happy to lend a hand. Such assistance was particularly appreciated when it came from a seller of an image that was too expensive for me to buy the actual hard copy, or conversely when it was from a buyer who ended up paying more for their item because I had been bidding against them. It is heartening to know just how decent most people can be and I have mentioned them all in the acknowledgements list. I have had generous donations and communications from other people as well but have to limit myself here to those who have in some way actually contributed to this book.

And so to the contents …

There are plenty of publications full of images of Guildford as it was in days gone by. I own at least ten of them myself! The biggest problem in constructing the book was in finding images that have not been used before. Yes, my collection is vast and includes plenty of rare and costly pictures but often that picture will have been used in someone else's work. As far as is possible I have tried to avoid any duplication of photographs that have been used by my predecessors. This really cut down the possibilities initially as I had envisioned constructing a piece primarily of Guildford 100 years ago. During the meeting with the other collectors I learnt a valuable piece of advice which opened up a huge new vista: people are, in fact, more keen on seeing Guildford as it looked in *their* past. Far from overlooking parts of my collection from the 1950s and beyond, I should have been picking these images out as the most important of all.

As the owner of this book, you will probably know some of Guildford's history. It was founded about the year 500 on a prehistoric trackway and a Saxon town grew up around the area of the current St Mary's church. The Norman castle was founded shortly after 1066 and the town grew in medieval times, as it became rich on the wool trade. After a downwards trend it started to grow again as an overnight stop on the London to Portsmouth route and expanded considerably after the arrival of the railways in 1845. Industry continued with Dennis, Drummonds and various breweries. The town is now rightly considered to be one of the most picturesque (in places) market towns in the South and is still the County Town of Surrey even if the administrative centre has moved to Kingston. The famous Guildhall clock is said to be the third most photographed clock in the country (after the clock tower of the Houses of Parliament and the Eastgate clock in Chester).

I am delighted to be able to share my collection with you and I thank my publisher for so readily agreeing to print my second book for them. I hope in these pages you will find some things you didn't know, some places changed beyond recognition (and hopefully more that haven't), maybe some people from your past and – most importantly – some memories that had become fuzzy round the edges, brought back into clarity by seeing an old image you didn't know existed.

Philip Hutchinson,
August 2006

one

Guildford Castle

Left: The castle keep from the south-east as it looked in 1885. Guildford Municipal Council had just acquired it from Lord Grantley. The banks are still in use as vegetable plots, and the Tudor brick window on the east side of the second floor has collapsed. This would be repaired before it opened to the public in 1888.

Below: A rare view of the castle grounds, almost certainly from the winter of 1888. The shrubs in the foreground have only just been planted and there is, at this stage, no sign of the public baths in Castle Street that were to open in 1889.

The interior of the castle keep from the east from a postcard view, *c*. 1905. The building still looked much like this when it closed for renovation in 2000. The one notable difference was by that time the caged doves seen here under the staircase had long since gone, to be replaced with countless nesting pigeons. The doorway to the left of the cage at the top was only discovered in 1887 and unblocked in 1888.

The interior north wall of the castle keep in the 1910s. This view can no longer be obtained as the building has now been refloored and reroofed. The roof level now cuts right across where the man is standing on the second floor.

FROM
THE CHAPEL
GUILDFORD
CASTLE

Jeffery & Sons, the sports shop in the High Street, owned a pair of miniature cannon which were fired on special occasions from the cage on the roof of the keep. Though small, they are remembered as being very loud!

Guildford town centre as viewed from the cage on top of the keep, c.1910. Apart from the distant spire of St Saviour's there is virtually nothing in this view you can clearly discern today.

The ante-chapel in the castle keep as it looked in the 1910s. This chamber is covered in carvings hundreds of years old, many dating from the time the building was used as the county gaol. The blackening of the chalk was caused by centuries of pollution. It was cleaned in 1998 and this thankfully removed a lot of the superficial modern vandalism, which post-dated this view.

Bandstand. Guildford Castle

Valentines Series

The bandstand in the castle grounds, *c*.1900. Though the structure itself has changed little since it was built in 1888 there are several differences in this view, most notably the later terracing and shelters which now lead down to the bowling green.

The cannon seized in the Boer War sitting at the entrance to the castle grounds (Tunsgate is off left and the bowling green is off right). At one time this cannon was positioned on top of the motte in front of the castle keep.

The bowling green and castle keep in 1934, clearly showing the chimney from the Castle Street Public Baths on the right. The baths came down in 1971 and now Eleanor Court and a strip of open grassland mark the spot where they stood.

The Bowling Green, Castle Grounds, Guildford.

An Edwardian view of the bowling green. The houses on South Hill behind still stand but the green itself is in a far better condition these days – just look at those bare patches in the foreground!

The bowling green and the old house which stood at its side in 1902. The house was formerly a pub named the Bowling Green Inn. It shut in 1887 and then became the head gardener's residence. It was finally pulled down in 1938.

The War Memorial was placed where you see the sundial in the previous view in 1921. In this image from Coppard & Kester of Guildford you can just see the Boer War cannon behind it to the left. In 1994 a smaller memorial to those lost in the Second World War was unveiled between the two Doric columns.

In 2006, razor-sharp pampas grass in the castle grounds might well lead to lawsuits! This early Edwardian view shows the bottom part of the gardens looking towards Chapel Street. You can just see the much-missed fountain (in many ways, Guildford's own Euston Arch!) right of centre.

The Castle Grounds, Guildford   4034

There are two major differences today in this view. Firstly, at the time of writing the old fishpond which had been filled in at various stages was on the verge of restoration. Secondly, there was a time when visitors could walk inside the early thirteenth century extension to the King's Chambers – this archway on the right is now locked up and the room beyond is used as a giant compost heap.

There is a very familiar view of the fishpond featuring these girls, but this is a rarer image. This view dates from 1905 and shows you just how big the pond once was. The interesting fountainheads were discovered in the filled-in pond as when they were disabled they were simply cut off and thrown in.

The castle gardeners laboriously sweeping the path free of heavy snow in The Valley of Flowers down towards the King's Chambers at an unknown date – possibly during the snowdrifts of December 1927 but maybe as early as the 1910s; even the clothing is difficult to date here.

Looking out from the extension to the King's Chambers in the middle of the twentieth century into the main part of the castle grounds. Again, this is a view a photographer would currently be unable to recapture.

Right: The old artificial waterfall in the motte of the castle as it looked in the late spring of 1963. It was inactive by this time but still remained in situ until the late 1970s. Beneath you can see the old fishpond. It seems there might have been a water shortage!

Below: The path around the motte then – as now – planted with daffodils as it looked after the Big Freeze of 1963 had finally disappeared. This path has been closed for some years and in 2006 is in desperate need of conservation.

A brass band – possibly from The Friary – plays on the bandstand on a Sunday afternoon in 1963. In those days the staff would put out deckchairs and the audiences would be larger than they are now.

The Valley of Flowers during the harsh winter of early 1963. Beyond you can see the roof of Holy Trinity church.

A lone figure braves the elements in this perfect view of the motte and King's Chambers taken early in 1963.

An old albumen print of Castle Arch taken in 1888. The major change here, of course, is the construction of the gallery to the new Guildford Museum along the left-hand side of this picture in 1911. In other respects this has not changed a great deal in 120 years.

INTERIOR OF CASTLE ARCH, GUILDFORD.

The entrance to the office of the Surrey Archaeological Society in the early 1900s. At that time, families still lived in the other parts of the building, both the east wing of Castle Arch (built c.1600) and the cottage beyond on the right. This cottage still exists but the whole wall is now blank and hung with tiles and the whole building is shared with Guildford Museum.

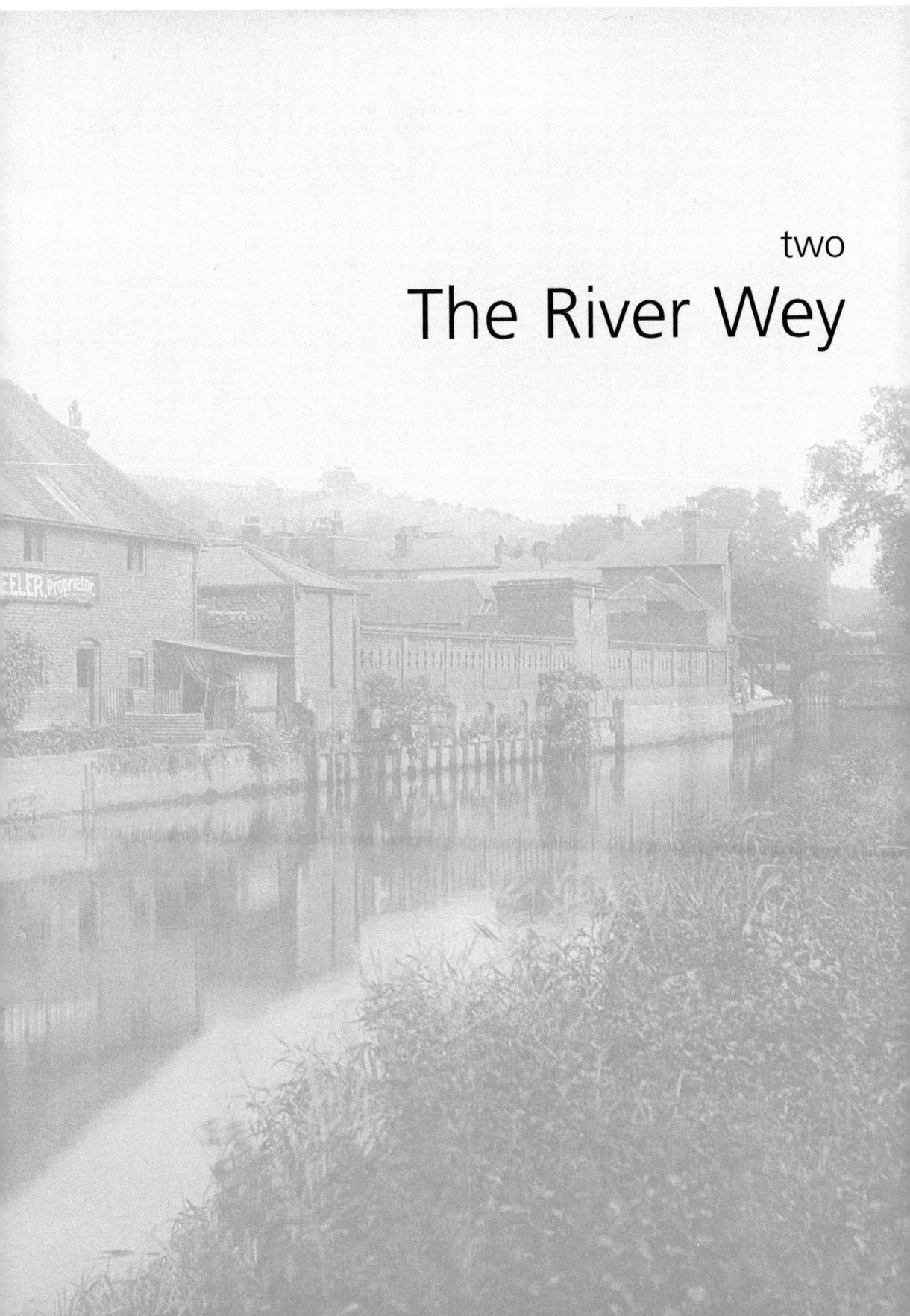

two

The River Wey

Guildford clearly showing Holy Trinity church, the semaphore tower, the Castle Keep, St Mary's church and the Victorian St Nicholas' church in 1842. The river in the foreground looks wide and shallow here. This was engraved from the spot where only a couple of years later Guildford Station would be built.

When you hear people speak of floods in Guildford, most people would think of those in 1900, 1928, 1968 or 2000. However, the town has seen plenty more breaches of the River Wey than these. These pictures from the *Illustrated London News*, for example, show floods in the town in 1877.

A very different time! There are at least six boats in this Edwardian view of the River Wey under St Catherine's Hill. The hill, of course, is now partially subsided and much overgrown. The building on top of the hill is The Beacons.

The famous St Catherine's Ferry in use, c.1900. The ferry service continued on a less regular basis until the 1960s. Now there is a modern bridge spanning the Wey at this spot so there is no call for such a facility. The cottages still exist, but now look different due to the addition of a large gabled wing on the left-hand side.

It would be almost impossible for a layman to identify this spot today. This is the River Wey at the bottom of the town centre, taken in 1895 from the spot where the YMCA is now. You can see Wheeler's Mineral Waterworks on the left (where the Electric Theatre stands today), and Warwick's Bench and the

old town bridge in the distance. Nothing here, except for the treadwheel crane next to the bridge on the opposite bank, survives.

The 'new' town bridge in the 1910s, taken from where The White House stands in 2006. The medieval bridge was destroyed in the floods of 15 February, 1900 and the new one, which remained until it was replaced in the 1980s, spanned the river following its opening on 5 February, 1902.

Tumbling Bay, just outside the town centre to the south, as it looked, c.1900.

Quarry Street looked very different in 1900! Half the buildings (those on the right) were demolished in the 1960s as the roads were rebuilt and all these gardens beyond now lie under the A281 road to Shalford. Someone's been doing a lot of washing!

A century-old view that can only really be traced today by the still-surviving tree on the left with the curving trunk. At one time, the small peninsula near The Jolly Farmer pub was full of houses. Now it is an open picnic ground giving no idea of the previous buildings. Who could imagine sheep in the town centre today?

This view has changed but is still clearly identifiable as the small island between the Millmead Council Offices and the Yvonne Arnaud Theatre. A hundred years ago there were no beer cans on the ground and the youngsters had nothing more sinister to do than look at the fish.

Millmead at a time when the road stopped at The Mill, and long before the Yvonne Arnaud Theatre was built to the right. St Mary's church lies beyond. (*Chris Quinn collection*)

The River and Locks, Guildford.

Just to the south of the town, about where the modern Council Offices stand now, looking towards the locks at the end of Millmead. Edward Beeney of No. 18 High Street published this card.

On the back of this card bought from the post office in the High Street someone has written, 'We hired a boat here and went for a row'. This view post-dates 1913, when the Jolly Farmer pub in the middle was rebuilt in this style. In fact, this view has not changed a great deal beyond there being far greater tree cover today.

All these buildings were demolished around 1960 for the construction of Millbrook. In this late 1950s picture it appears that the River Wey has burst its banks and is flowing quite aggressively.

Stoke Park with cows? Surely not! You would be forgiven for not recognising this spot. Behind the large tree in the middle is Stoke Mill, now home to the *Surrey Advertiser*. The field on the other bank is now the A3. This view by Youngs of Guildford comes from the late 1900s.

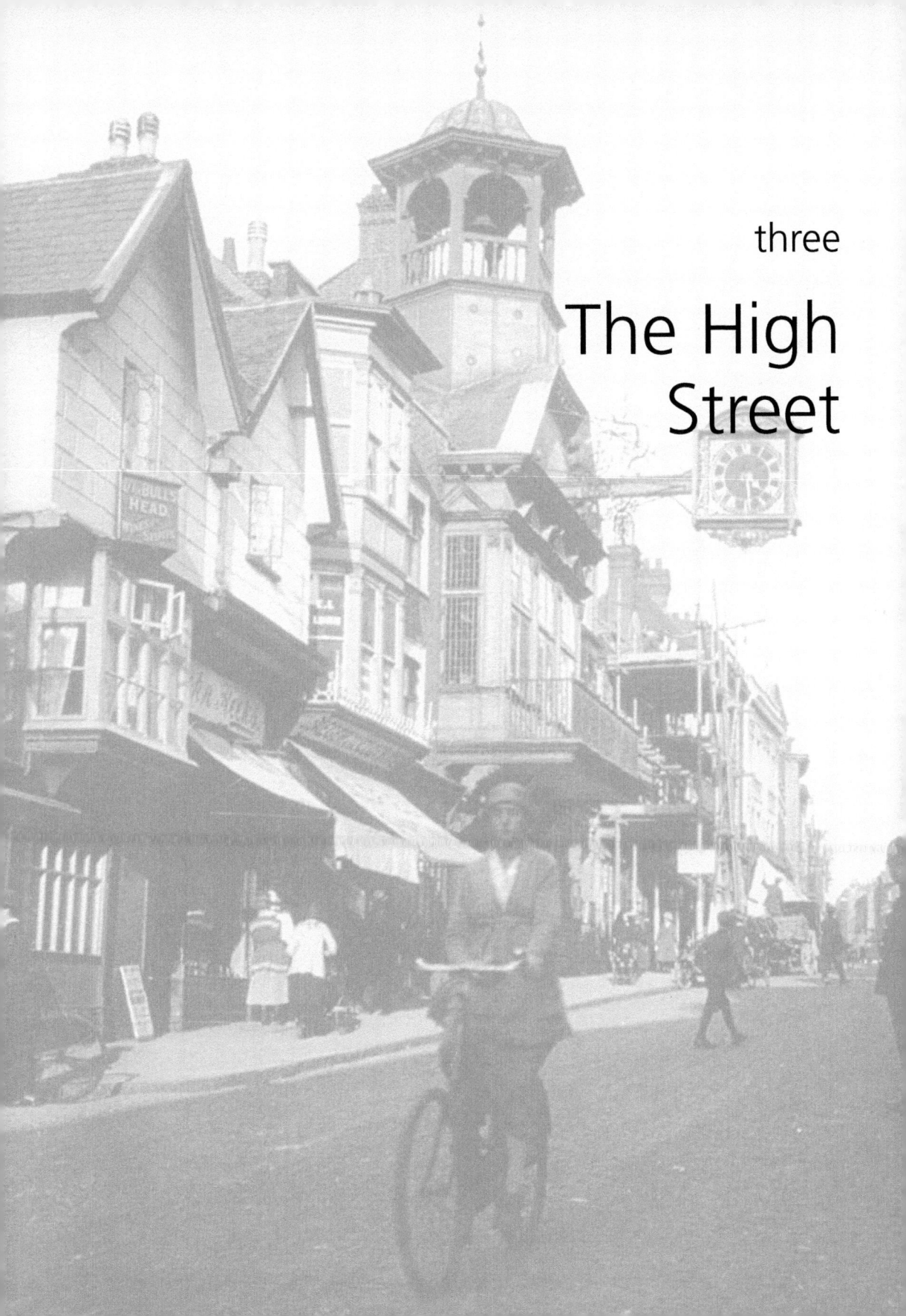

three

The High Street

Guildford High Street in 1895. All of society is here. The gentrified man and his daughter on their charges in the foreground, the coachman, the footman discussing matters with the trader, the schoolboy, the shopkeeper – even a dog. Beneath the lamppost in the centre you can see a street

orderly's barrow for cleaning up the masses of transport by-product! At a glance this is instantly recognisable as Guildford High Street in the twenty-first century if you add 100 more people and a few dozen cars. There are many changes but these are subtle.

Street musicians play at the entrance to Bury Street in front of St Nicolas' church, *c*.1900. Busking in Guildford was probably not as popular a century ago as it is now, though anyone playing for cash on this spot would probably not get much custom today.

The Jubilee Arch placed over the Town Bridge on George V's Silver Jubilee in 1935. It only stood for a week and some locals were disgruntled it cost £115 to construct. This was once a popular habit in the town and it would be nice if such things were done today. Sadly, society now is such that it probably would be a Jubilee ruin within a few days. (*Julian Morgan collection*)

Just after the war years and the High Street is snapped from the roof of St Nicolas' church. The buildings in front came down when Millbrook was built. At that time Wingrave Clark, the estate agents & auctioneers, occupied the building under the advertising hoarding. Just look at the grim austerity of the structure on the left behind the white frontage of the Lion Hotel (demolished 1957).

Compare this image to the large one from 1895 on the previous page and you get an idea of increased traffic. This picture of the High Street was taken halfway between the Victorian photograph and today, in the late 1950s. The photographer would now be standing in the middle of the busy A281 to take this. On the right you can see Jackson's Garage which many people will well remember.

An open coach making its way down the High Street in 1925, just on the corner of Quarry Street. Not an uncovered head in sight!

Looking down the bottom part of the High Street in the 1940s, shortly before the pinnacle on top of St Nicolas' church was removed and replaced with a shallower point on the tower in 1951. The Lion Hotel is clearly seen on the right. The buildings on the left look just the same today as they did then although the pavement is a lot wider at the Quarry Street junction.

Woolworth replaced The Lion Hotel and opened in the town in 1958. This and the following two images come from a staff magazine published at the time. The original White Lion from the old hotel is visible behind the shutters on the left.

Still quite a novelty at the time, a well-stocked food hall like this would have been very popular. It is still old enough for a sign to instruct people that this was a store with modern self-service.

Above: Prior to opening, this is the canteen in the Guildford branch of Woolworth. Anybody want to buy a utility bowl and spoon for 1s 6d?

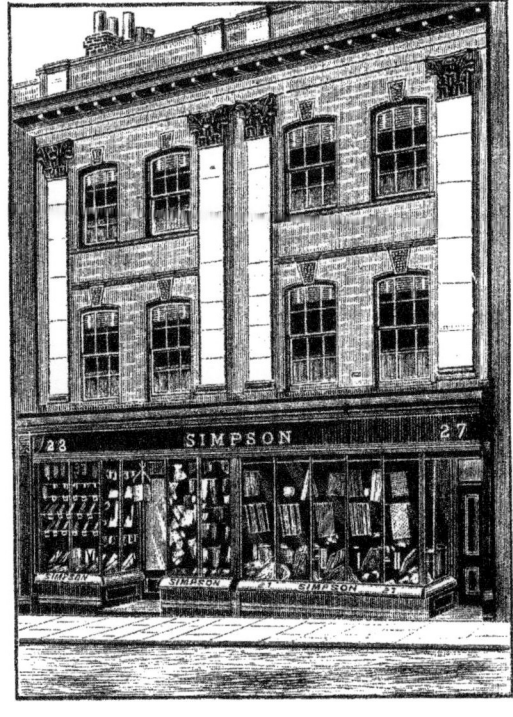

Above: The entrance hall to the Lion Hotel as it looked in the second half of the 1920s. Publicity material claimed it dated from 1593 and Samuel Pepys stayed there. Bedrooms were *en suite* with sitting rooms and a banquet hall. The hotel was lit by electricity and also had a spacious billiards room and a motor and cycle house for the use of visitors.

Right: Simpson Bros shop from a Guildford guide of 1896. It says, 'The premises at the above address in High Street compromise a very commodious and handsome building, with plate glass windows, and containing 2 fine shops. Mr Simpson is an enterprising and courteous gentleman, possessing sound experience of a thoroughly practical character'.

Opposite below: Angel Yard behind the ancient Angel Hotel in 1963. The yard still looks very similar today, though now filled during the summer months with alfresco diners. In 1963 you could still park your car there.

Looking up the High Street from the junction with Quarry Street, *c.*1960. The curious thing here is that most of the shops visible on this view are still in business and many of them still trade in Guildford, though few from the same premises. On looking at the traffic you can see just when post-war austerity came to an end. The amount of cars and people nearly half-a-century ago almost equals that of today.

Looking up towards the Guildhall in 1906. Just beyond the back of the coach on the left you can see the shop of M.C. Cheel, the tobacconist and cigar merchant. Contemporary publicity stated, 'Since commencing business, Mr Cheel has earned for this house a well-deserved popularity by reason of the excellent quality in tobaccos'. He was also the sole agent in Guildford for Farnham Ales, which were known for their, 'excellent properties and exceedingly moderate prices'. Cheel's remained there until the 1950s.

A recently discovered image that will bring back a lot of happy memories! Inside Lyon's Caterers in Guildford in 1963. The business was there by the 1930s and continued until the late 1970s. It served the young of Guildford on the spot where Superdrug stands in 2006, halfway between The Angel Hotel and Market Street.

At the old road crossing near Market Street in 1963. A lone workman is replacing some setts in the road. On the left can be seen such shops as Faiman and Fifth Avenue. The building next door with bay windows on the first and second floor is the much-missed Corona Café.

The staff of the International Tea Stores in 1926. It would be impossible to identify this location were it not for old town directories. This is the spot where Phones 4 U has their shop today. Unlike the impression you get from many old images, the staff here seem to be by and large a happy bunch.

You would be forgiven for thinking this group photograph predates the one above, but it is actually around 1930 by which time the business had expanded premises, being refronted and taking on the shop next door. The impressive building today that appears to have ancient Tudor brickwork zigzagging across its front and possibly Jacobean carvings looked nothing like that in the early part of the twentieth century. From left to right: Laddie Varall, Miss Ward, Miss Trussler, Miss Harper, Mr Merritt, Miss Trussler, Mrs Rickton, Kitty Knight, Daisy Stemp, Mr Harper.

The photographer Donald Birkenshaw photographed much of Surrey in 1948. This view shows when lights still precariously hung across the street. Cheel's tobacconist is still in residence next door to the International Tea Stores, by this time having the frontage with which we are all familiar.

Father Christmas walks down the High Street in December 1973. His young assistants are advertising a jumble sale that morning at 10.30 a.m. at Holy Trinity church. This was taken just opposite Tunsgate Arch. (*Brian Ireland collection*)

Left: The Guildhall in the mid-1920s. A cyclist makes her way down the hill as a policeman looks on. The Bull's Head pub is on the left and next door is the shop of John Reeks, gone by the 1930s. At Russell House further up the street some extensive repair work is taking place.

Below: The council chamber in the Guildhall, c.1905. There has been a guildhall in Guildford on this spot since medieval times but much of this building is from 1589 and beyond. Though not generally open to the public, this private meeting room looks much today as it did a century ago with the exception of the furnishings. At the time this image was taken criminal cases were still heard at the Guildhall.

Opposite above: It has just been pouring with rain, as is evident on this 1902 view of the High Street outside the White Hart hotel (demolished in 1905 to make way for Sainsbury's). Note the high ladder next to Russell House on the other side of the street. Health & Safety executives would not be impressed!

Below: And this is the interior of the building that replaced The White Hart in 1906. Not bearing much similarity to the Sainsbury's Central standing on the same spot one hundred years later, this far predates the bizarre notion of filling a basket by yourself.

Guildford House built by John Child is today the home of Guildford House Gallery and looks much the same both inside and outside as it did in antiquity. For many years it was the home to the popular Nuthall's Caterers when it was still numbered No. 25; the High Street was renumbered in 1960. (*Julian Morgan collection*)

The ornate surviving staircase in Guildford House. Today the pictures in the building are grander in style and presented in a more professional manner!

St. Abbot's Hospital, Guildford

Above: From the High Street, Abbot's Hospital looks exactly the same now as it did one hundred years ago. Very little here has changed except for the destruction by arson of the building on the far right in 1916. The hospital was founded by George Abbot in 1619 as a retirement home for elderly Guildfordians and was modelled on the great gatehouse of Hampton Court Palace.

Right: This photograph from the late 1950s would look no different now. A perspective not often seen by most people, this is inside the private courtyard of Abbot's Hospital looking out to the central steps of Holy Trinity church beyond.

Above: The Trinity Taxi Rank captured in 1963. This little wooden hut had a far longer lifespan than most people realise – almost one hundred years. It was put up in the late 1800s and was only taken down in the 1970s by which time it was commonly referred to as the Cabmen's Shelter. It stood between the central steps of Holy Trinity church and the smaller staircase to its left.

Opposite below: Looking from the top of the main part of the High Street, *c.*1902. The Cabmen's Shelter is clearly seen underneath Holy Trinity church but of more interest are the buildings on the right. The Three Pigeons can be spotted before the 1916 fire that destroyed much of it, and closer towards the viewer are buildings that were demolished in 1913. Most notable is the old High Street Post Office and Library, with sagging trestle tables of old books out on the street.

Right: The demolition of Ram Corner itself in April 1913. This spot was the narrowest point on the main London to Portsmouth road and it was decided that The Ram Inn and the buildings around it had to come down. The curve of the road where it joins onto North Street and Chertsey Street now occupies this area. (*Judy Oliver collection*)

Below: The Upper High Street (as it was then known, having previously been named Spital Street) in 1906. Much of the right-hand side of the street could just be recognised today, but nothing remains of all the buildings on the left.

Further along Upper High Street at about the same time. The ubiquitous policeman stands outside the Royal Grammar School on the right. On the left behind the railings once stood Allen House. This was pulled down and replaced by the modern 1960s main building of the RGS.

The Old Smithy, High Street, Guildford.

Though this may look like it could be at the junction of Swan Lane, the ramshackle old Smithy was actually on the spot where McDonalds stands near the top of the High Street now. It was inherited by Richard Lymposs from his father in 1880 and shut in 1906, shortly after this photograph was taken.

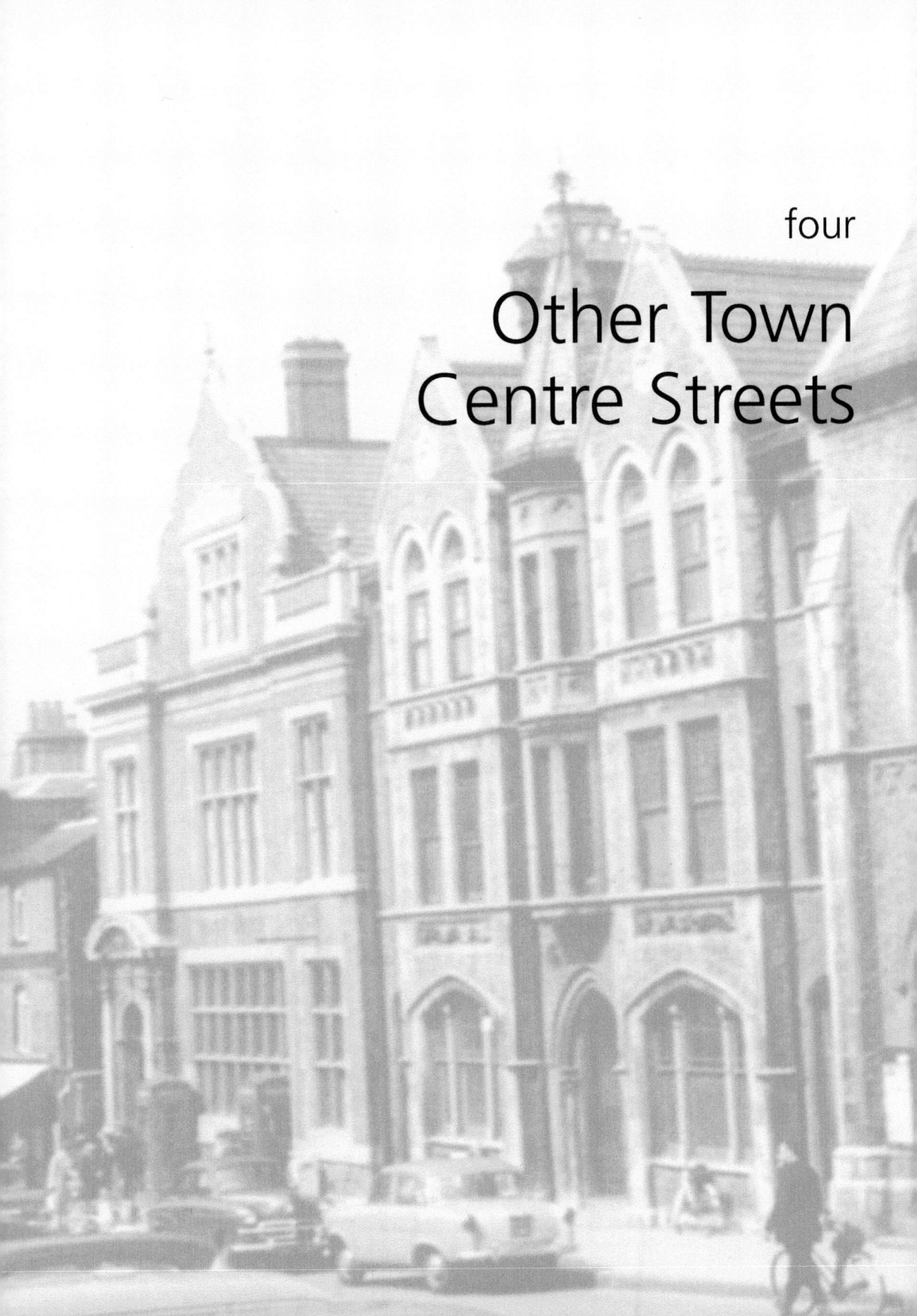

four

Other Town Centre Streets

An exciting discovery! This pencil sketch by G. Walker comes from a scrapbook dated 1845 and is titled simply, 'MM's residence, Guildford'. Research has found that this house stood in Portsmouth Road and was the property of the spinster Macaulay sisters, who are listed as being local 'notables' in *Russell's Town Almanac* of 1848.

Possibly the quintessential image of lost and lamented Guildford. These cottages stood in Park Street since Tudor times yet were scandalously ripped down in 1956 in the cause of progress. Such a thing would never be allowed today – or would it?

Half a decade later in 1961 the site is still vacant. Only the doorway of the leftmost cottage remains. A.H. Pyle of the Guildford Camera Club cannily recorded these photographs.

Again in 1961, this is the station side of the cleared site still awaiting development. Curiously there is a large collection of bicycles, prams and other furnishings on the right hand side.

The demolition of the chimney at the Friary Brewery in 1973. The brewery had been a huge success story, not least because of its policy of buying up all the smaller breweries it could find. It was finally taken over itself by Ind Coope in 1969 and now the whole area lies underneath the sprawling Friary Shopping Centre.

Following the demolition of the brewery, archaeological excavation began. Dozens of skeletons dating from the time of the original thirteenth-century Dominican Friary were uncovered and those that were found were eventually reinterred in St Mary's Churchyard in 1987. This burial was uncovered in 1978 and could clearly be seen in situ by the public. (*Lucy McCorkindale collection*)

An inspection of the Second Royal Surrey Militia (who were stationed at barracks at the bottom of North Street and on the site of the old Friary) by Colonel Bushe in Woodbridge Road on Friday 2 June, 1854. The Mount can be seen rising up above and the second St Nicholas' church stands on the far left. Following the inspection of seven hundred troops, Col Bushe retired to a meal at The White Hart in the High Street with 200 guests.

The functional Guildford Sports Centre, built in Bedford Road in 1971 and here captured in 1974. It eventually came down in the 1990s as the area was regenerated and The Spectrum Leisure Centre outside the town superseded it. The modern Guildford Odeon now stands on this spot.

Quarry Street in the late 1920s looking rather as it does today. St Mary's church is in the middle of the picture and part of The Star pub is on the far right. This card was published by T. Pallot of No. 1a Commercial Road.

A miraculous survival. Though the gardens have been lost under Millbrook, the house on the right has had a modern extension added and the one on the left has been reroofed, this view taken of the rears of some of the houses in Quarry Street otherwise looks much as it did fifty years ago.

The purpose-built display gallery of Guildford Museum, constructed in 1911. This room has itself now been entirely rebuilt and houses the shop and early Guildford history galleries. Most of these items have now spent years in storage.

The ironwork gallery in the Museum in the 1920s. This room is on the first floor and is where you will find the display case of old tiles and an ornate fireplace. The mind boggles to think how the staff would manage to deal with exhibits displayed in this way today!

Left: The ornate Victorian doorway of Quarry Hill House which still survives, though the owner has told me she has caught tourists prising studs out of the door! Quarry Hill House has a superb back garden with substantial remains of the old castle, which the public do not see. J. Beyerlein who traded at the other end of the street sold this postcard.

Below: The town from Rack's Close, *c.*1920. No sign of the busy A281. St Nicolas' church is clearly visible and just rising out of shot on the left is the Hog's Back.

Above: Rack's Close in the 1930s when it was still classed as part of a pleasure garden with appealing rustic fences and benches. Nowadays a modern steep metal staircase descends down a sheer wall and only dog walkers and underage drinkers seem to frequent the area.

Right: The entrance to the mysterious Guildford Caverns in Rack's Close in 1930. Long since blocked up, these chalk quarries provided much of the clunch chalk for the buildings in Guildford Castle. Public tours used to take place of the caves but the fragility of the chalk and the damp conditions have led to huge crags the size of grand pianos to break through and hang dangerously over the paths. However, they have been occasionally opened up to gather chalk to replace pieces ripped out of Castle Arch by careless drivers.

Left: The original North Street Post Office. It was built in 1886 and demolished in 1971 and occupied the site of its replacement, which itself moved to the junction with the High Street in 2006.

Below: North Street in 1963. Almost all of this view has gone. The Wesleyan church stood where Barclays Bank is now, the old post office is in the centre and on the right is the Congregational Hall, which came down in 1965.

Opposite above: David Boxall, a passenger on a traction engine, was killed in an accident on Epsom Road on 9 February, 1911 when the driver lost control at the criminal speed of 12mph. The barrier has not prevented a large group of onlookers inspecting the wreckage.

Opposite below: Epsom Road at its junction with the High Street during the Big Freeze of early 1963. The original Guildford Odeon, opened in May 1935, can be seen on the right. Above the awning is written, 'The home of entertainment is here!' though sadly it is impossible to read what film was playing at the time.

Fatal Smash Epsom Road, Guildford 9th Feb 1911

The Hunt meeting in Dene Road on Boxing Day 1953. An image belonging to a different time. One Guildfordian told me that her family used to watch the hounds set off each year but they weren't aware of them ever killing anything. (*Brian Ireland collection*)

Another image by A.H. Pyle of the Guildford Camera Club showing the open car park behind Holy Trinity church in Sydenham Road in 1960. This was during the short hiatus between the demolition of the previous old houses that stood there and the ghastly multi-storey car park that replaced it, now itself thankfully no more than a bad memory.

five

Outside the Town Centre

Guildford from The Mount around 1900, showing buildings no longer standing. The bottom half of the street has been rebuilt but the top cottages remain. This view could not be obtained today as it is right on the top of the sheer chalk face dropping down to the railway line and has been fenced off for years. The spot is now totally overgrown with trees.

Hillier's Almshouses still stand directly to the west of Farnham Road Hospital. This card dates from the end of the First World War and the sender has written to the recipient in Somerset, 'What do you think of these Almshouses? Some difference to the ones at home'. The Earl of Onslow gave the land here and these almshouses opened in 1879.

The exterior of The Royal Surrey County Hospital (now Farnham Road Hospital) as it looked from the site of the current Guildford County School one hundred years ago. The building has hardly changed at all. It was opened in 1866 and Florence Nightingale herself was consulted about the design.

An interesting unknown celebration in a women's ward at Farnham Road in 1907. This card was sent to a Mrs Allen of Martha Ward in Guy's Hospital, London and the writer has sent the message, 'All patients send love to you'. Whether Mrs Allen was a nurse or patient we don't know.

Left: The exterior of Hillcote, which was recently identified as being a house on the Mount side of Wodeland Avenue, in 1916. The house has changed little, but the one on the right has long since been demolished and Nether Mount now climbs up in its place.

Below: The residents of Hillcote and their dog in the back garden, taken at the same time. This second part of Wodeland Avenue (after the junction with Wherwell Road) was newly built as can be seen from the lack of grass. Judging from other images in the series, it was probably about early spring. This may well be Mr and Mrs W.G. Ricketts who were resident at the address several years later.

Opposite above: This garden has now changed in many ways. Behind Hillcote, Mareschal Road and Mount Side have now built upon the whole hill. The rockery, filled with masonry spoil in 1916, has now been removed and a lower level patio is in its place. Tribe & Robinson, who also built the first part of Wodeland Avenue in 1906, built this row of houses.

Opposite below: The living room in Hillcote is remarkably similar today. All that has gone is the original fireplace. The windows and beams are still in situ. A copy of the *Daily Express* lies on the armchair and plants, ornaments and photographs were very much the order of the day.

Guildford station from Guildford Park Road, as it looked in the 1950s. The railways came to Guildford in 1845 and this original station building was finally pulled down and replaced in 1988. A few of the buildings you can just see beyond in Walnut Tree Close survive, but the old gas works are long gone.

A Class N 2-6-0 arriving at Guildford from Redhill on 15 April, 1963 with the obligatory train spotter on the right. Beyond is the old roundhouse, which finally came down in the 1970s and now has a large multi-storey car park in its place.

Farnham Road and St. Nicholas Church, Guildford.

Farnham Road would be virtually unrecognisable in this Edwardian image were it not for the sight of St Nicolas' church beyond. This is the stretch of road beginning in Park Street and continuing to the Hog's Back. The station is behind the photographer. All the buildings on the left had come down by 1972 as part of the road-widening scheme and even their replacements have now gone.

This card of the cattle market was sent from a woman who had just visited her father in the Royal Surrey Hospital in 1908. Guildford's cattle market moved from North Street to the Woodbridge Road site in 1895. The police station and law courts now stand on this spot.

Woodbridge Road, looking towards Woking, as it appeared, *c.* 1905. The terrace of buildings on the right still remain and at the time of writing are undergoing extensive refurbishment. The entrance to The Leas can be seen on the left and behind the trees was Dapdune Crescent, now the cricket ground.

A very interesting image. This CDV, probably from the 1870s, ended up in America. It was taken by W. Bassett of No. 37a Stoke Road so it is fairly safe to assume it is of a pair of cottages in that area. However, the positioning of them does not match any two houses in that part of town by the time of the 1895 Ordnance Survey map so it is likely they came down shortly after this photograph was taken.

A diesel train passing over the bridge at Stoke in 1925. The Stoke Hotel can be seen on the left. The cottages on the right have now gone and Regal Court now occupies the spot. Beyond the bridge is Stoke Park Gardens. (*Julian Morgan collection*)

Stoke Park Gardens – originally called the Jubilee Gardens – were acquired in 1889. This 1930s view has not really changed a great deal. A Japanese bridge still spans the (toy) yachting pond but a lot of the area is not treated with the same respect past Guildfordians gave it.

The Guildford Lido, almost as popular now as it was when this image was taken, shortly after its opening by the Mayor of Guildford, William Harvey, in 1933. Harvey was responsible for having been principle fundraiser for the Lido and his speech and inaugural dive into the pool were recorded – with sound – by news cameras.

Manor Way at the time of its construction in Onslow Village in 1920. Lord Onslow sold the land for the post- World War One estate for only twenty-five per cent of its value and some of the houses were ready by the end of the year. (*Bev Williams collection*)

Few people realise that the Guildford bypass dates from the same time as the Lido in 1933, the Lido in fact being built on the side of Stoke Park so the roads could give convenient access to it. This card by Judges shows part of the bypass shortly after it was opened. (*Chris Quinn collection*)

A view of the A3 Guildford bypass taken looking north from the bridge on the A31 Farnham Road in the middle of the 1950s. The cathedral is clearly visible in the distance; its tower still as yet unbuilt. Incredibly, much of this view survives in an undeveloped state.

The Womens' Royal Army Corps depot in Stoughton in 1964 when it was largely rebuilt in a more modern style. The whole area has now been rebuilt as a housing estate called Queen Elizabeth Park.

The dining hall at the WRAC depot as rebuilt, looking very stark and utilitarian.

The recreation room at Stoughton looked no more appealing, but at least they had a television set and matching furniture.

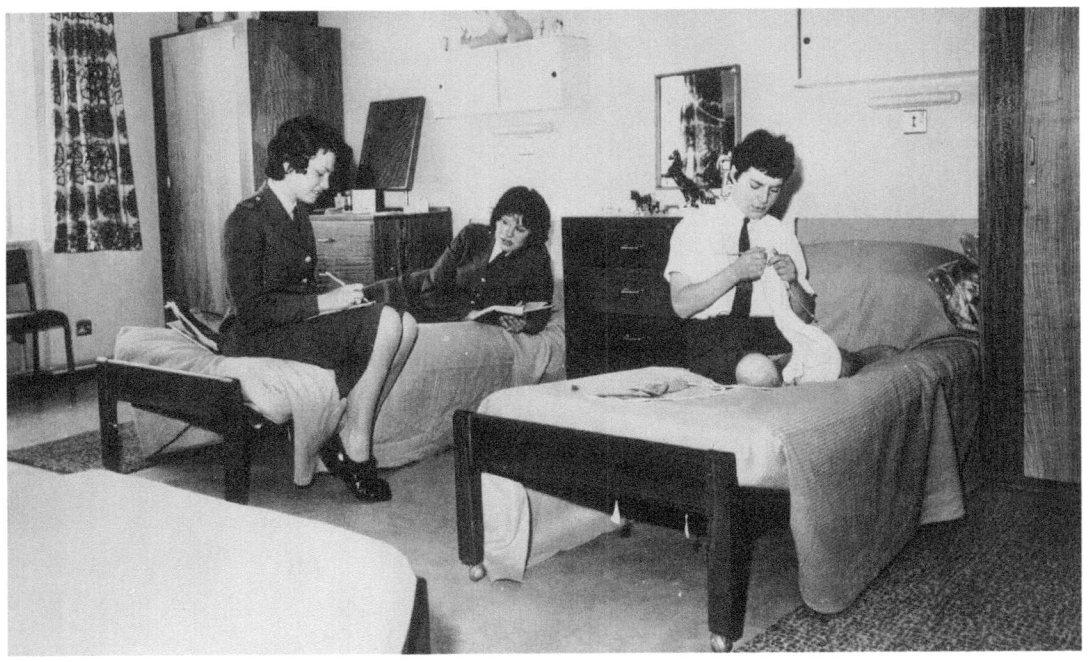

The depot at Stoughton (not to be confused with Stoughton Barracks) was originally built during the Second World War as a training camp for the ATS. Nothing remains of either period of depot buildings now. Here three young recruits pose desperately – and vainly – trying to make the place look exciting.

Stoughton Barracks, home of the West Surrey or Queen's Regiment, in which the author's grandfather served during the First World War. Cardwell, the Secretary of State for War, selected this spot which had previously been open fields. These buildings and the imposing Cardwell's Keep at its side (off to the right of this shot) have been regenerated and preserved as a successful and exclusive housing development.

The entrance to Abbotswood, just off London Road, in the 1930s. The road still looks similar today but the foliage around the archway and the plants along the edge of the pavement have gone.

Merrow Village Green just before the First World War. The sender of this postcard is anonymous, but they were staying at Merrow Croft and wrote home to Derby, 'This is such a lovely place. I have never seen anything so pretty before. Having such a good time. Am going to London again tomorrow. You would so like it. I shall not want work after this.'

Fairyland is a name now lost to history. Though Rudyard Kipling wrote a poem about Merrow Downs he did not allude to it. No one seems to know where this spot off Trodd's Lane is, as the Downs cover such a huge area. This view is from the early 1900s.

In some ways this view looks as you would expect Shalford Road to have looked 100 years ago. The entrance to The Great Quarry is on the left with Chantry View Road further down and Shalford Park on the right. This card was sent from London to Scotland from a woman who mentions her husband's new motor car.

A very familiar moment but a rare photograph of The Great Storm that battered Guildford on 2 August 1906. A tree fell through the roof of these surviving cottages on Shalford Road, narrowly missing a seventy-eight-year-old man named Mr Comber sleeping next door. This view was sent to an ill child living on Farnham Road only a month later.

The Congregational church outing to Shalford Park in 1912. Everyone in their finery to have an afternoon 'out' just a mile from the building in North Street!

Ice skating on the water meadows at Shalford Park. At times in the past, when the water level was high, parts of Shalford Park were flooded from sluice gates on the Wey to create a natural ice rink in the winter. Here, during 1963, this remained well into what should have been spring.

Above: This dramatic late 1930s image of Warwicks Bench above The Great Quarry was sent into the heart of the Third Reich. It shows just how close the houses are to the side of the sheer chalk face.

Below: Echo Pits, now more commonly called the Great Quarry, in the early 1900s. Quarrying died out here in the 1880s. It was used as a rifle range by 1902 but by 1921 it failed to meet its reserve at auction. It was finally turned into a small estate of fifteen houses in the later 1920s. (*Chris Quinn collection*)

Echo Pits, Guildford.

Right: The spring and Ferry Lane at the foot of the River Wey looking up towards St Catherine's Hill in the 1930s. The spring was said to hold miraculous curative properties and is still exposed today with a sham bridge and seat by it, but it wouldn't be recommended to bathe your eyes in it anymore.

Below: A fascinating piece of Guildford's past. This 1910s card of St Catherine's Hill clearly shows the large Victorian House called The Beacons, which was destroyed by fire in 1974. The plateau where the house sat is now at the top of the car park leading from Portsmouth Road. Nothing remains of it except some steps and fragments of the garden wall, now totally overgrown and halfway down a very steep slope to the River Wey at the bottom.

View from St. Catherine's, Guildford.

Above: Another 1910s view of St Catherine's looking over as yet undeveloped land towards Guildford with the Great Quarry clearly visible. The cottages beneath still exist but are now obscured by trees

Below: St Catherine's Village looking back towards Guildford, *c.*1905. The Ship Inn, still going strong, can be seen on the right. Though the road looks very different now, this view is fundamentally unchanged.

St. Catherine Village, Guildford

Right: Sandy Lane is a long and rural road that stretches from St Catherine's Hill towards Loseley Park. It is less confined today but scarcely more built up than it seems on this picturesque yet slightly creepy view from 1910.

Below: A meeting of the hunt on the Hog's Back, *c.*1900. At that time the road to Farnham was still a single carriageway. This picture was taken standing on the junction with Puttenham Road.

Meet of Hounds on The Hogs Back, Near Guildford.

An hilarious image from the mid-1920s of the Hog's Back (still single-laned) looking towards Farnham and showing the worst excesses of the once popular art of postcard découpage. The car and picnicking family on the left were cut and pasted from elsewhere. This explains how two parents and six children could fit into a car that could only seat a total of two children.

Quite different conditions in this shot! Here we see a Lymposs & Smee delivery van stuck in deep snow on the Hog's Back on 28 December, 1927 taken by D.E.H Box of Guildford. The question needing an answer here is how did Mr Box get so far outside Guildford in such deep snow to take this photograph in the first place?

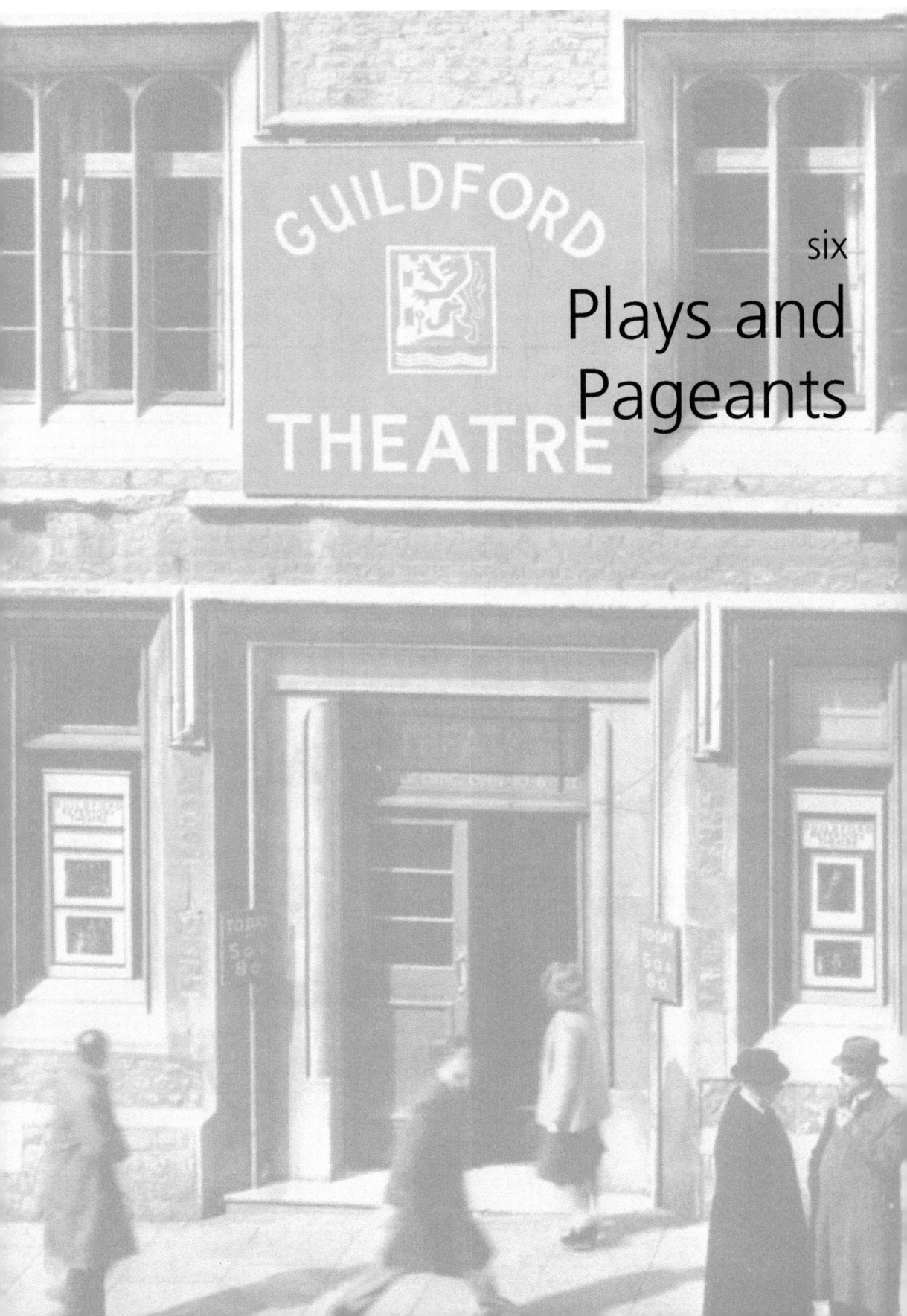

six

Plays and Pageants

THEATRE, GUILDFORD.

BY DESIRE AND UNDER THE PATRONAGE OF THE

ALDERMEN
AND
TOWN COUNCIL.

Miss MARY GLOVER
The Last Night but one, of her Appearance.

On THURSDAY EVENING, OCTOBER 16, 1851,

The Entertainments will commence with the admired Drama, (in two Acts), now playing with great success at the London Theatres, entitled—THE

FACTORY GIRL;
Or, All that Glitters is not Gold.

Sir Arthur Lastell Mr A. NELSON   Jasper Plum Mr R. LOCKWOOD   Stephen Plum Mr C. HUMPHRYS   Frederick Plum Mr H. VEZIN
Toby Twinkle Mr T. FRY   Harris Mr TUCKER
Lady Leatherbridge Mrs BARNETT   Lady Valeria Westenleigh Miss FRANCES
Martha Gibbs · · (the Factory Girl) · · **Miss MARY GLOVER**

IN WHICH SHE WILL SING,

A NEW BALLAD, CALLED "THE VALLEY."

PAS SEUL BY MISS THOMASSIN.

To be followed by the Comedy of

PERFECTION;
OR, THE LADY OF MUNSTER.

Sir Lawrence Paragon, Mr R LOCKWOOD.   Charles Paragon Mr HUMPHRYS.   Sam, Mr T. FRY.
Kate O'Brian - - **Miss MARY GLOVER.**
Susan, Mrs BARNETT.

WAPPING OLD STAIRS, MISS FRANCES.

COMIC SONG "LORD LOVEL," MR. T. FRY.

The whole to conclude with the Petite Comedy of—THE

TWO QUEENS.

George Collet Mr C. HUMPHRYS,   Magnus Buter, Mr T. FRY.   Burridge, Mr A. NELSON.   Servant, Mr TUCKER.
Mary Queen of Denmark, Miss LOVE.
Christiana, Queen of Sweden (disguised as **Count Donbar**) **Miss MARY GLOVER.**

On FRIDAY, for the Benefit of Miss MARY GLOVER, her last Appearance
this Season,—"The Dream at Sea." "Apartments." and "The Pet of the Petticoats,"

A rare playbill for the Guildford Theatre, which used to be halfway down the west side of Market Street. It was opened in 1800 and Edmund Keane played there in 1843. It had a single small entrance but could seat four hundred audience members. This playbill was for 16 October, 1851. The theatre shut in 1889.

THEATRE
ROYAL
GUILDFORD

Photo by Coppard & Barton

A Buffet is attached to each part of the Theatre where Wines, Spirits, Bass and Guinness, Cigars and Cigarettes of choice brands, also Chocolates, may be obtained.

BIDDLES LTD., PRINTERS, GUILDFORD.

The front cover of a programme for the Theatre Royal in North Street when *Ruddigore* was performed there in the early 1920s. It opened in 1912 but shut only twenty-one years later due to its shortcomings in meeting fire regulations. Argos now occupies the same spot.

Above: An image from the historical pageant held at the Royal Grammar School in 1910 demonstrating discipline in the classroom during the early years of the establishment. Today the roles are more likely to be reversed in some schools!

Below: A super posed photograph of the Royal Grammar School's production of Shakespeare's *Henry IV, Part I* in 1924. Here we see a scene at the Boar's Head Tavern. From left to right: L.R. Hawkins, R.O. Jenkins, E.C. Evans, H.H. Gillingham, L.H. Clarke, J.T. Doctor, S.B. Girling.

Right: The cover to the script of a major Guildford pageant play from 1925 called *The Town of the Ford.* The pageant was co-narrated by the Saints Martha and Catherine, who both gave their names to well-known Guildford chapels.

Below: Boys from the Royal Grammar School perform the piece *Traffic of the Ford* in the 1925 pageant on the bowling green at Guildford Castle. This scene can be identified as being a short piece involving King Alfred the Great.

Left: The Labour politician and later Mayor of Guildford Leslie Codd, who wrote the 1940 Guildford pageant *This Precious Stone*. The pageant was later filmed using members of Guildford's youth groups in 1946 and though stills from this production have been discovered, the actual film remains a Holy Grail for Guildford historians.

Below: The entrance to the Guildford Theatre in North Street in 1948. The theatre was converted from the Borough Halls, next door to the now unfeasible site of the original Theatre Royal but it was destroyed in a huge fire in 1963.

Opposite above: A scene from *Nothing but the Truth*, a comedy set in a New York stockbroker's office, performed at the Guildford Theatre in 1946. Left to right: Kenneth Osborn, Richard Voss, Allan Barnes, Jonathan Meddings.

Opposite bellow: Lally Bowers as The Queen in *The Eagle Has Two Heads* which was a huge success when produced by Peter Potter at the Guildford Theatre early in 1948.

Left: Roger Winton, who was the first resident director at the Guildford Theatre from when it opened in 1946. Winton trained at RADA and had been involved with repertory theatre for some years when he came down to Guildford. He had also worked on television and radio in the late 1930s.

Below: Still going strong forty years after this photograph was taken in 1968, David Clarke has always been known as Guildford's Master of the Pageant. He has been involved in these public spectacles for over half-a-century and was one of the founder members of the Cloister Players in 1958.

Opposite above: Malvolio making a fool of himself in Rack's Close during the Cloister Players production of Shakespeare's *Twelfth Night* in July 1960. David Clarke directed this production.

Opposite below: Sir Toby Belch and Sir Andrew Aguecheek plotting with Maria in another scene from *Twelfth Night*. These photographs were taken by A.H. Pyle and exhibited at the Guildford Camera Club in 1961.

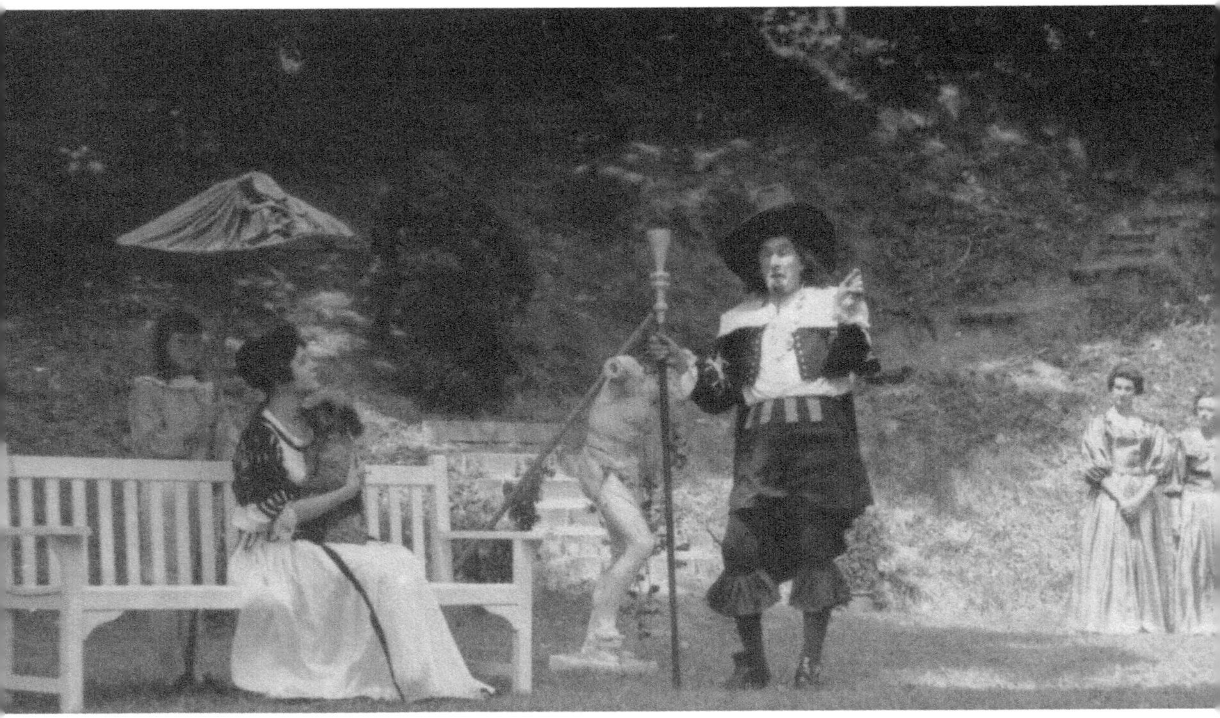

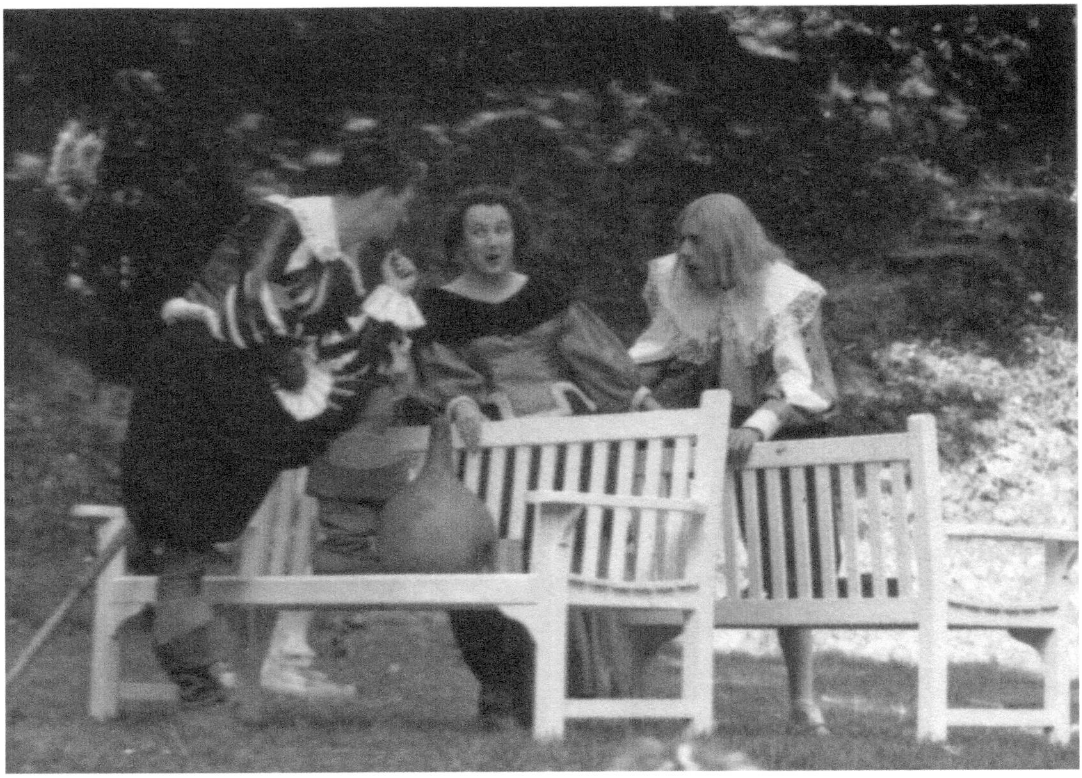

Sir Michael Redgrave starting the machinery that began construction of the famous Yvonne Arnaud Theatre on the banks of the River Wey in October 1962. Whilst teaching at Cranleigh School in the 1930s, Redgrave used to be involved in amateur dramatics in Guildford.

Throughout the construction of the Yvonne Arnaud Theatre, celebrities were often invited to take part ceremoniously for the press. Here we see Susan Hampshire applying bitumen to the roof on 11 November, 1964. The theatre opened seven months later and remains one of the most highly respected receiving houses in the country, hosting many productions before they successfully transfer to the West End.

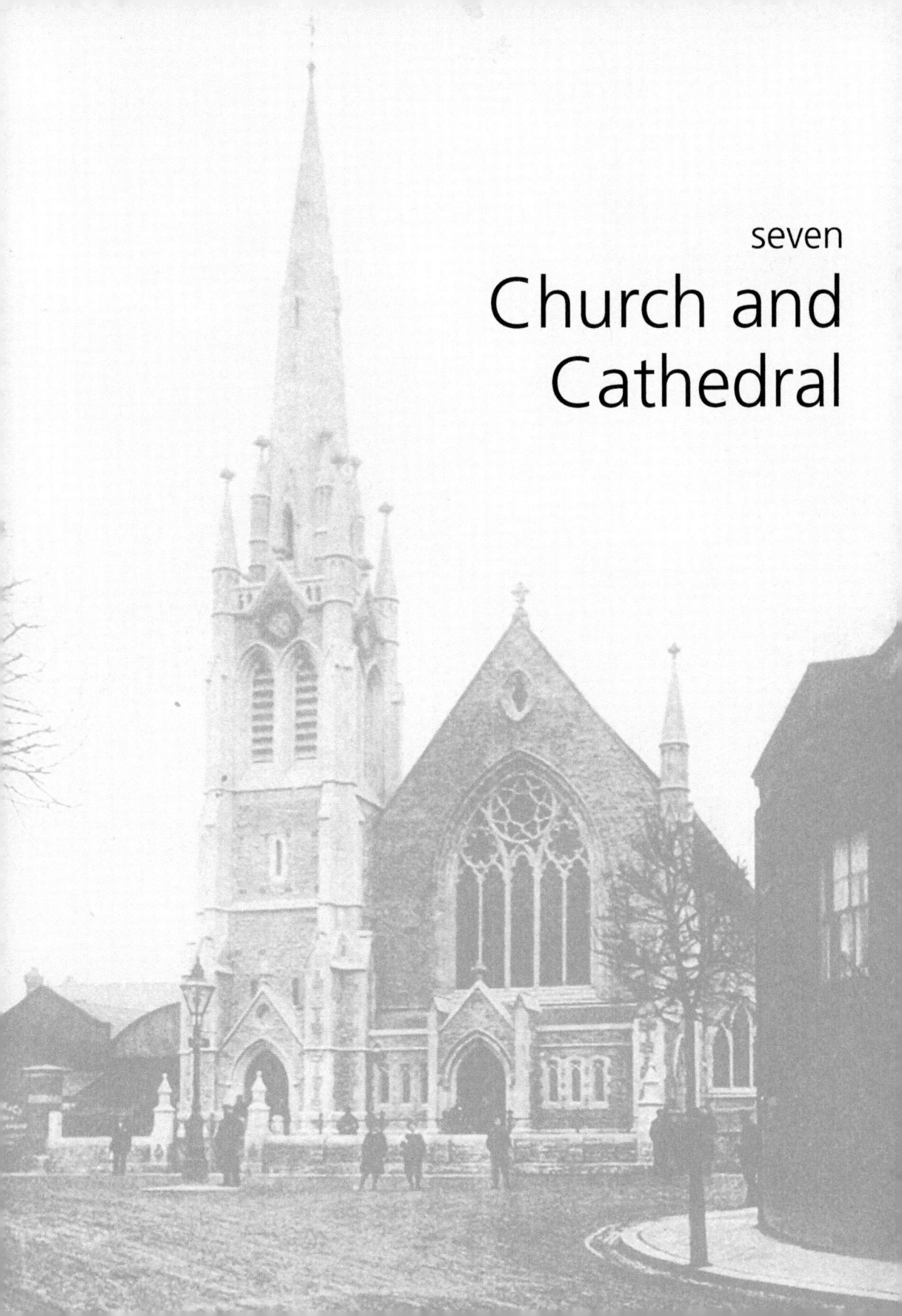

seven

Church and Cathedral

The Kingdom of Jesus Christ:

In Answer to some Points treated of, in the Rights of the Christian Church.

IN A

SERMON

Preach'd before the

Right Reverend Father in God,

JONATHAN

Lord Bishop of *Winchester,*

AT HIS

PRIMARY VISITATION

AT

GUILFORD, July 5. 1708.

JOHN XVIII. 36.
Jesus answered, my Kingdom is not of this World.

By WILLIAM WHITFIELD, Chaplain in Ordinary to Her Majesty.

Publish'd by his Lordship's Command, at the desire of his CLERGY.

London : Printed and Sold by *H. Hills,* in *Black-fryars,* near the Water-side, For the Benefit of the Poor. 1708.

Above left: The cover of a printed sermon given by William Whitfield in front of the Bishop of Winchester at Guildford (commonly Guilford as seen here) on 5 July, 1708. Unfortunately it is not known which church was used for its delivery. The chapbook covers sixteen pages of very small close type and appears to be a protestation against seemingly heretical reforms, so no change there then.

Above right: A charming little watercolour of the second St Nicholas' church (1836-1874) poorly designed by Robert Ebbels but retaining the tower of the original medieval building. G. Walker executed this painting on the banks of the River Wey in 1845.

Opposite above: St Nicolas' church in 1906 taken from the junction with Portsmouth Road. Though variations on the spelling still abound it is thought that the church lost the 'h' from 'Nicholas' around 1880. Samuel Teulon designed this church at the request of the rector of the church, John Monsell. Both men would die before it was completed, Monsell himself following a fall from the roof on 9 April, 1875.

Opposite below: The beautiful St Nicolas' Rectory on Portsmouth Road in the 1890s. It was built as Rookwood House in 1835 and extended in 1863. Two gardeners are hard at work. Sadly the rectory came down in 1973 – another wonderful piece of architecture gone forever.

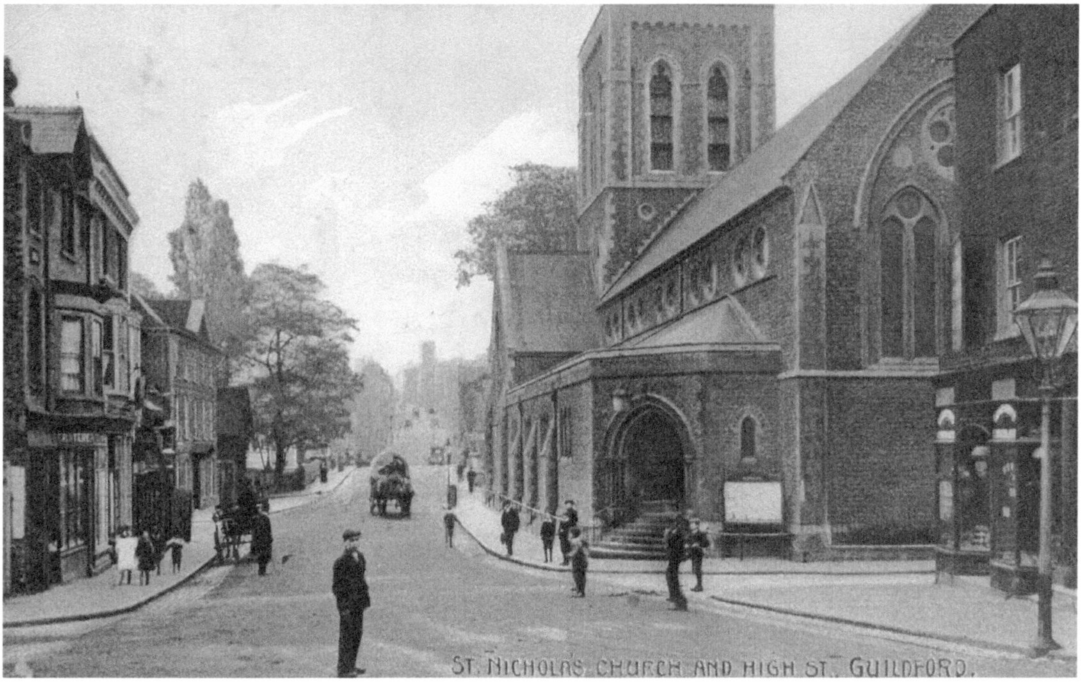

ST. NICHOLAS CHURCH AND HIGH ST. GUILDFORD.

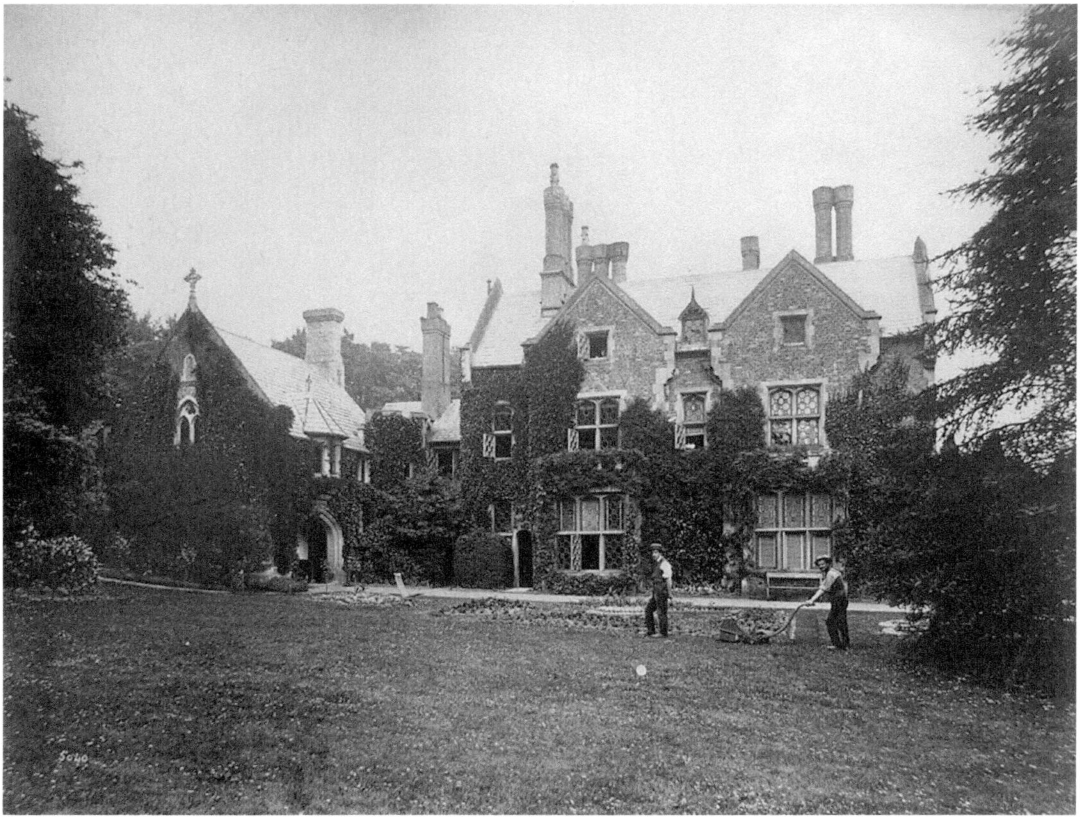

An unusual angle of St Mary's church in Quarry Street in 1913. The tower of St Mary's is almost 1,000 years old. Some of the gravestones have now been removed and several trees cleared. The sender of this card was staying as Prospect Villas in Harvey Road, yet in spite of this not being the closest place of worship they have written, 'This is the exterior of our church'.

Holy Trinity church in Edwardian times. It became the Cathedral church in 1927 until the building on Stag Hill was opened. This church dates from the middle of the eighteenth century. One small thing that has baffled Guildford historians is why was a double-thickness brick wall being built in front of the steps on the bottom left?

A drawing by Alfred Pearce and published in *The Sphere* newspaper of the unveiling of the Boer War Memorial in Holy Trinity church in July 1902. Thirty-one Guildford men were commemorated on the plaque. Mr Broderick, a Minister of State, preached a sermon beforehand.

Possibly one of the most missed buildings of Guildford's past; the Wesleyan church in North Street in the early 1920s. This Methodist church replaced an earlier Victorian building (1844-1892) and the impressive structure was finished early in 1894. It came down in 1973.

The exterior of the original St Joseph's Catholic church in Chertsey Street in the early twentieth century. It was built in 1884 and was only demolished in 1982 when a new church around the corner in Eastgate Gardens replaced it.

The altar of St Joseph's Catholic church in the late 1900s. Lanhams of Stoke Road took this view, based just yards away from where the church used to stand.

St Saviour's church on Woodbridge Road as it looked in 1906. The church is virtually unaltered today but the buildings on the corner are long gone. This card was sent just after it opened and the sender indicated they were staying just opposite the church, which would have put them next door to the cattle market. Two men had been participating in dares to ascend the tower at the time this card was posted!

Christ Church in Waterden Road in 1904. It was consecrated in 1868 but wouldn't be finished until the twentieth century. It still looks the same today. The sender of this view has written, 'Just arrived here. Staying for two days to recruit health – Temperance Hotel again'. That structure still stands on the corner of North Street and Ward Street.

Right: The late 1930s and the chancel of the Cathedral of the Holy Spirit, being constructed on Stag Hill, is virtually unrecognisable. Some postcard sellers have even claimed this is the result of bomb damage in the Second World War!

Below: The crypt of the cathedral just before the war and awaiting the fittings that would turn it into a chapel, which would be dedicated in 1947. For some time this chapel was used as a parish church.

G.8639.   CRYPT LOOKING WEST FROM NORTH ENTRANCE, GUILDFORD CATHEDRAL.

The construction of the nave at the cathedral in the 1950s. Massive fundraising exercises were undertaken in the time of post-war austerity and the position on top of the hill meant that for years people could see – and hear – the work going on from the town.

George Reindorp, the 5th Bishop of Guildford from 1961-1973, with scouts and guides outside Guildford Cathedral in the early 1960s. Reindorp was known to have been very fond of young people and wrote various accessible books on religious instruction for them.

The foundations of the cathedral, designed by Sir Edward Maufe, were lain down in 1936 and 1937. Following years of inactivity during the war, work starts again on completing it in 1952.

A prized ticket for the Pilgrimage to Guildford Cathedral at Easter 1955. Hundreds of people attended this great publicity drive to get the building completed. Princess Margaret was guest of honour and the 3rd Bishop of Guildford, Henry Campbell, led the service.

GUILDFORD CATHEDRAL PILGRIMAGE
17th April, 1955

Parish   Shalford.

Name   Mary Hirst.

Coach Letter   A.67.

Coach Number   This Coach will pick you

Coach Park up at The Jolly Farmer at
Southway Avenue.)   12-45
Cars are parked in roads designated by the A.A. according
to the colour of your Ticket.

LOOK FOR YOUR DIRECTION INDICATOR
ON LEAVING THE CATHEDRAL SITE

This Ticket admits you to the service and must be retained
throughout.

Many Guildfordians will remember the cathedral with its tower unfinished. Though the cathedral was officially consecrated in 1961, it was not until 1963 when work was finally completed. This picture was taken in 1958. To the right you can see the original cross marking the site. It was made from ship's timbers and, misunderstanding this, at least one local boy assumed this was a mast and an entire ship was buried underneath the cathedral!

From one structural extreme to the other. The remains of St Catherine's chapel built by Richard de Wauncey, the rector of St Nicholas' church, in the early 1300s as a 'chapel of ease' for parishioners who lived too far from Guildford to make the trip into town each Sunday. It has been a ruin for centuries and still sits serenely on St Catherine's Hill, whilst trains roaring through the tunnel underneath shake the ground.

eight

Education, Education, Education

This could be a very important local photograph. It came from a collection of Guildford images but the photographer had their business miles away in Esher. The background looks very similar to other photographs known to have been Stoke Infants in Markenfield Road. Sadly, the blackboard at the front has faded so as to be unreadable. However, on the original image it is just possible, in the right light, to make out the first two letters as 'ST'. This may, of course, just mean 'Saint', but if it is 'Stoke' then this image from the late 1860s is probably the oldest known photograph of Guildford schoolchildren.

Again, another wonderful image and possibly the author's favourite in this book. The football team of Archbishop Abbot's School for the 1908-09 season. This spot is still recognisable as being behind the Edinburgh Woollen Mill in Jeffries Passage. The school closed in 1933. Some of these students, particularly the captain, can be identified in a school photograph from several years previously (*in Guildford: A Pictorial History* by Shirley Corke). It is a sobering thought to realise within a decade many of these boys would have found themselves in the trenches of the First World War.

The exterior of The Royal Grammar School in the early 1960s. This sixteenth-century building is now used less by the school since the construction of a modern set of buildings on the other side of the street where Allen House once stood.

The Headmaster's Lawn at the rear of The Royal Grammar School in 1922. (*Jo Harle collection*)

The courtyard of the original 'Big School' in 1922 still looking the same today as then, though the uniform has changed considerably and the modern blue blazers are a very familiar site in the town. Contrary to popular opinion, the school has not always had a secure future and indeed was in financial difficulty when this photograph was taken. (*Jo Harle collection*)

The interior of the main schoolroom in 'Big School' in 1922. The beams, complete with the painted names of famous ex-pupils from history, and the fundamental structure of this room remains the same today. The formal rows of desks, however, are no more. (*Jo Harle collection*)

The winners of the Junior Challenge Cup of the Surrey Secondary Schools Swimming Association in 1922. These grammar school boys are, left to right: S.B. Girling, E.F Fox, C.P. Williams, K.S. Fox, C. Ives. Girling can also be seen on the far right of an image from the school's production of *Henry IV, Part I* (page 90).

The Under 14 XI of the grammar school in the 1922-23 season when they won the Guildford Borough Schools League Championship. Back row, left to right: A.J. Humphreys, D.E. Tyrrell, W.F. Hancock, Mr Jones, C.P. Williams, G.F Lyon, W.H. Hensby. Middle row: J.S. Milton, R.R. Broatch, L.D. Gates (Capt.), E.H. Gerrard, G.H. Wheeler. Front row: T.H. Parkin, G.E. Wilson.

The Royal Grammar School First XI of 1922. Back row, left to right: Mr Lank, R.H. Hill, C. Fenby, A.A. Milford, H.N. Godfrey, R. McCormack, Mr Bowey. Middle row: K. Lee, W.E. Philpott (vice-Capt.), J.A. Broatch (Captain), D. Copus (Hon Sec), T.W. Ford. Front row: K. Roberts, J.J. Watkins.

The First XI look very different in this 1971 photograph by P. Norman Button of Castle Street. Back row, left to right: R.J. Stedman, A. Dick, A. Harris, J. Thorpe, N. Gillingham, D. Nind, P. Pay, A. Dart (scorer), W.H. Hore. Front row: G. Forbes, G. King, R. Otter (Capt.), D. Atridge, D. Sweet.

Stoke Park school in the mid-1920s. At this time Mr and Mrs Charles E. Lewis ran it. The Georgian mansion was demolished amongst much outcry in 1977 and a skateboarding park in the corner of Stoke Park Gardens now marks the spot.

The Inner Hall of Stoke Park School as it looked in 1922. The staircase was a very fine one and it is a great shame the building was lost when you see how grand the interior was. In its final years it was used by Guildford Technical College, who now occupy newer buildings a few yards away. (*Jo Harle collection*)

The seniors' classroom at Stoke Park in 1922. Not quite as grand as that at the Royal Grammar School but still impressive. The Lewis's offered, 'Special and complete preparation for the Public Schools, the Royal Navy and all examinations. Every pupil entered for the above has been successful. Home life, individual tuition (backward boys a speciality), very careful moral training'.

The boys' dining hall in 1922. Formally set, but retaining airs of a family atmosphere as the Principals state in their advertisements. There's even a piano in the corner. (*Jo Harle collection*)

Stoke Park Concert, Lecture and Dining Hall from the same series of postcards published by P.A. Buchanan & Co. of Croydon. It goes without saying this is an impressive room!

'B' dormitory at Stoke Park School. Unlike the previous images, this kind of existence looks very Spartan and gave the boys no privacy whatsoever. There is a single unshaded electric light bulb hanging from the ceiling. (*Jo Harle collection*)

Above: A game of hockey in 'the Thirty Acres' at Stoke Park in 1922, though that name would soon no longer exist as a decade later the Guildford bypass sliced through Stoke Park and left the school with half its original grounds. (*Jo Harle collection*)

Left: Sunnydown School on the Hog's Back as it looked in the 1950s. Sunnydown was a school for, 'delicate boys' who either had learning or behavioural difficulties. The school moved to Carshalton in the early 1980s and the area has now been redeveloped as a group of houses called Compton Heights. Sunnydown Plantation, visible on the right, still remains however.

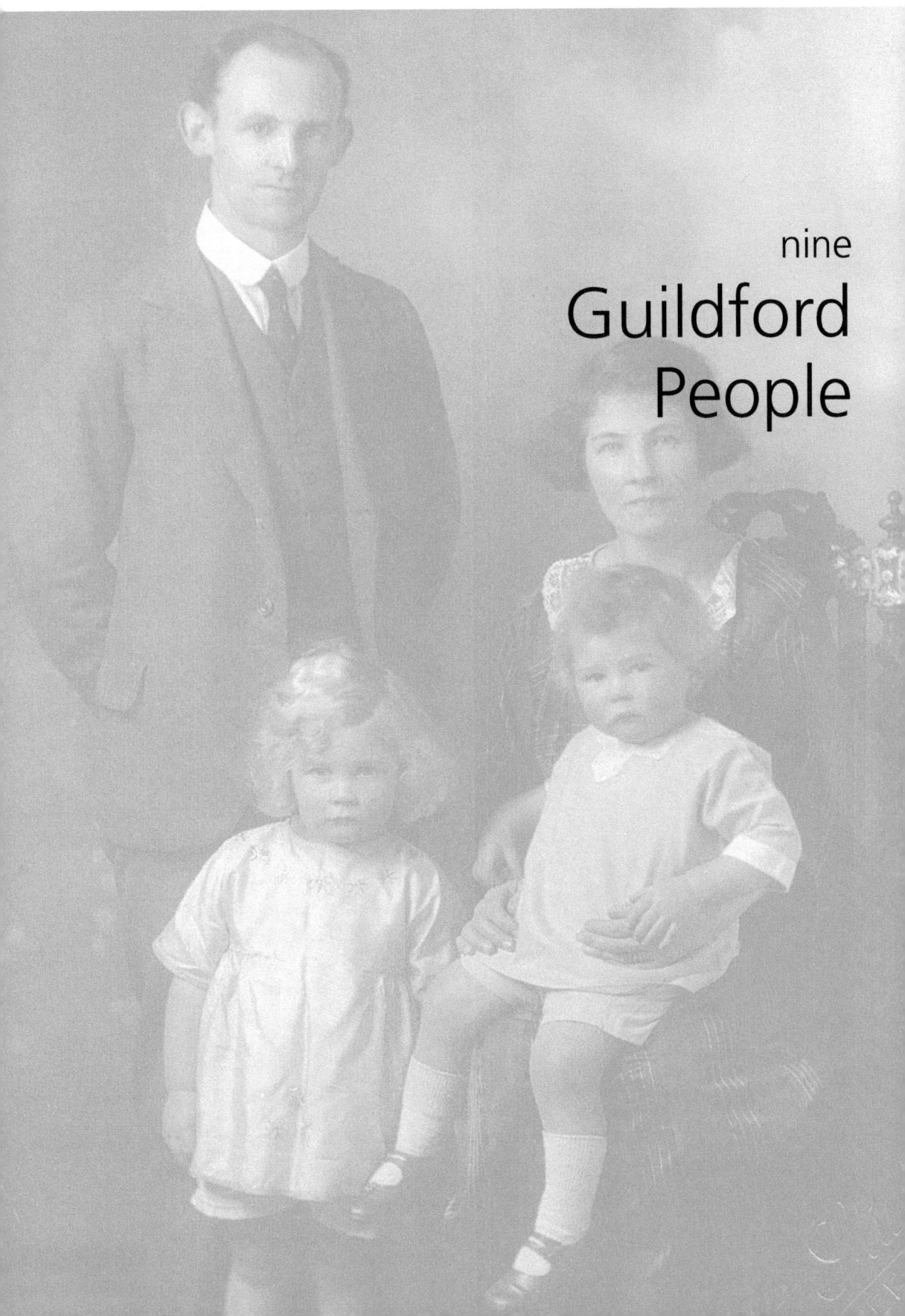

nine

Guildford People

An Indian Cavalry Officer on a *Carte de Visite* taken by the hugely prolific Drewetts of No. 47 High Street probably in the 1870s.

A typically formal CDV of a woman posing with props at the studio of E. Andrews whom was based at No. 50 Chertsey Street at the time. The company was not in Guildford at all in 1862 and by 1873 had moved to the High Street. They were gone by the 1880s. The hair and clothing, matched with this knowledge, dates this image to, *c.*1865.

A wonderful image of a little boy holding a splendid wooden horse in the days when boys were 'breeched' after spending their early years being almost unrecognisable from girls as they all wore dresses. By this time Drewetts had outlets in Basingstoke, Blackheath, Reigate, Dorking, Aldershot and Winchester. This card, like many others, has a reference number on the back. Tragically, the records of Drewetts and all the other studios are now lost. If only they could be found then all these people, and the date of their sittings, could be identified. This photograph would date to the late 1860s.

A larger cabinet card by Wheeler & Sons of Bridge Street of a young girl called Elsie, possibly taken for her first communion. It is likely Wheeler & Sons were not in business for long in Guildford and that this image dates to the late 1890s.

Above: Almost certainly R. Elliott, the milliner, dressmaker and fancy draper with his wife and mother in the garden of their house in Station Road, Shalford, in the early 1910s. There is no trace of Elliotts still being in business by 1930.

Left: A photograph taken by Drewetts of a gentleman called Ben and his family in December 1924. By this time the business had moved to North Street and was opposite the post office. I bet Ben never thought his family would find themselves in a book nearly a century later!

An individual that proved initially difficult to identify. This gentleman, looking very similar to the film director Mike Leigh, is actually Bishop George Sumner who became Bishop of Guildford in 1888 until his death in 1905. The idea that the first Bishop of Guildford was Dr Harold Greig, dating from the time when Guildford broke from the Diocese of Winchester in 1927, is not technically correct.

A signed card of the Bishop of Guildford succeeding Dr Greig, John Victor MacMillan (1934-49) who oversaw much of the initial construction of Guildford Cathedral and was consequently the first bishop to work there.

Above: The committee for the Coronation celebrations of King George V at Merrow in 1911. The trestle table in front is covered in small items, many of them with tags. These may well have been prizes.

Left: Ferdinand Smallpiece JP, a well-known Guildford benefactor of the time, in the early 1920s at a time when he was chairman of the governors to the Royal Grammar School. His family gave the name to the now-lost Smallpiece's Gateway, which used to be halfway up the southern side of the High Street.

Opposite below: The girls of the WRAC at Stoughton in March 1952 taken by Gwyer Gibbs of Pirbright. Though not identifiable here, some of the women who have signed the reverse of this image are: Kathleen Bly, Penny Bearham, V. Cheekley, Sheila Dowd, Jean Ellis, V. Holmes, Josie Greenland, Margaret Deegan, Ellen Hutchesson, Joan Gillis and Irene Gavin.

Above: Scouts from the St Saviour's Troop skinning a rabbit at camp on Ranmore Common in May 1947. The troop was formed in 1929 and by that time had 137 members in various divisions. Their HQ was at Shaftesbury Hall in Artillery Terrace.

Mayor Donald Wilkins JP, whose term of office covered the 1953 Coronation, in a photograph by Montague James. Part of Wilkins address read, 'The dedication of our young Queen to her great task will be in our minds throughout the day and during the festivities which mark the expression of our loyalty to her'.

The town crier, Jesse Peters, probably at the time of the Coronation in 1953. He is walking along Woodbridge Road. The Drummond Arms is just visible behind on the left. David Peters, the grandson of Jesse, is still the town crier today. (*Brian Ireland collection*)

Above: A group of policemen at Mount Browne in November 1951. This image came from the original collection of PC George W. Keeping, standing on the far right in the middle row. The men in the front row are, left to right: Inspector George Pentecost, Deputy Chief Constable Harold Back, Chief Constable Joseph Simpson and Chief Inspector Tom Farndale.

Right: Finally, we hit the year 2000. As part of the Millennium celebrations, staff connected with Guildford tourism became historical characters from Guildford's history in an event held in Castle Cliff Gardens on 1 July. The author is standing in the centre.

Other local titles published by Tempus

Leatherhead Then & Now

LINDA HEATH AND PETER TARPLEE

This collection of past and present images offers the opportunity to compare and contrast changing modes of fashion and transportation, shops and businesses, houses and public buildings, while recalling local people who once lived and worked in Leatherhead and the surrounding area. Highlighting some wonderful comparisons, this unique collection of over eighty-five pairs of images takes a nostalgic look back at life as it once was in Leatherhead.

0 7524 3680 5

Haunted Guildford

PHILIP HUTCHINSON

From heart-stopping accounts of apparitions, manifestations and related supernatural phenomena to first-hand encounters with ghouls and spirits, this collection of stories contains new and well-known spooky tales from around Guildford. Drawing on historical and contemporary sources, *Haunted Guildford* contains a chilling range of ghostly accounts sure to appeal to anyone interested in the supernatural history of the area.

0 7524 3826 3

Around Woking

LYNDON DAVIES

This fascinating volume of old images traces some of the developments in Woking during the 1920s and early 1930s. Drawn from the archive of Woking photographer Sidney Francis, this collection of over 200 photographs, many never before published, highlights some of the important events that have occurred in the town during this time, including rare views of Woking Football Club, officials at Brookwood cemetery and visitors to Woking Mosque.

0 7524 3230 3

Haunted Wandsworth

JAMES CLARK

Drawing on historical, literary and contemporary sources, this chilling selection includes the infamous Victorian murder mystery of Charles Bravo, poisoned one April night and still haunting the room in which he died, and the 'Poltergeist Girl of Battersea', who was haunted by a spirit who would follow her everywhere, even onto the bus! From the spectral son of Marie Antoinette to a haunting at the Battersea Dogs and Cats Home, this scary selection of ghostly goings-on is bound to captivate anyone interested in the supernatural history of the area.

0 7524 4070 5

If you are interested in purchasing other books published by Tempus, or in case you have difficulty finding any Tempus books in your local bookshop, you can also place orders directly through our website

www.tempus-publishing.com